T0011566

THE LITTLE BOOK OF
FISHING

Published in 2022 by OH!
An Imprint of Welbeck Non-Fiction Limited,
part of Welbeck Publishing Group.
Based in London and Sydney.
www.welbeckpublishing.com

Compilation text © Welbeck Non-Fiction Limited 2022
Design © Welbeck Non-Fiction Limited 2022

ISBN 978-1-80069-176-6

Compiled and written by: David Clayton
Editorial: Roland Hall
Project manager: Russell Porter
Design: Tony Seddon
Production: Jess Brisley

A CIP catalogue record for this book is available from the British Library

Printed in China

10 9 8 7 6 5 4 3 2 1

Illustrations: Freepik.com

THE LITTLE BOOK OF
FISHING

FISHERMEN'S TALES
FROM RIVER TO OCEAN

CONTENTS

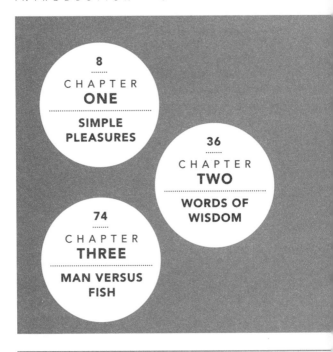

INTRODUCTION

Fishing. You're either in or you're out. And once you're in it's unlikely to be a short-lived affair or a flash in the (frying) pan. The joys of fishing are numerous and have been celebrated and well documented for centuries – probably longer if you count cave paintings. Mankind's use of fish as a foodstuff pre-dates any form of written history, but it is only relatively recently that fishing has existed as what we call a "hobby" (I use the term loosely – it's much more than that for most of us). It wasn't until we had the luxury of throwing a fish back in the water if we wanted that fishing became the pastime we know and love, because if you are under pressure to catch a fish – in order to feed your entire family for example – it's not quite the same as disappearing for a day or longer to sit around and contemplate life, the weather, and whether you packed the right bait, hooks or floats.

Few sports/hobbies/pastimes/obsessions (delete as applicable) captivate and mesmerize in quite the same way as humankind's quest to find out and then capture what lies beneath the surface of water, bring it out, weigh it and (frequently) just throw it back in again.

So from barehanded trout-tickling monks to the heaviest-laden recreational fisherman who leaves home with a trunk-full of expensive equipment, there is an affinity between man, fish and water that has been pondered upon for as long as we've been trying to separate those slippery creatures from their aquatic surroundings. Some of the greatest minds and literary giants have lent their theories on why fishermen do what they do, say what they say and live for time spent with the rod and line.

In the pages that follow, there are examples from the great and the good, from fishermen who see themselves as hunters, those who identify as philosophers, and those who simply want a bit of time alone. There are simple quotes, thoughts and passages that attempt to convey precisely what fishing is, why we do it, and what is so enjoyable. Some are long, some are short. Most are profound, many are hilarious, and I hope at least a few of them will strike a chord with those of you, who like me, enjoy the simple, silent challenge of fishing. And – as you would imagine, coming from fishermen – all of them are true…

CHAPTER
ONE

Simple Pleasures

What could be simpler than sitting with a rod and line in idyllic surrounds? This is the very essence of fishing in its purest form and why its global appeal has charmed millions of people for thousands of years. Peace, solitude and fish. What more could you ask for…?

66

A bad day of fishing is better than a good day of work.

99

Though the true author of the quote is unknown, the popular (and likely) theory is that it is derived from Sir Izaak Walton's *The Compleat Angler*. In it he theorized that *"A bad daye fishing always beats a goode daye of Worke"* (1653).

66

Work is for people
who don't know
how to fish."

99

Popular US bumper sticker, as quoted
in *The New York Times* (1987).

1,000,000
Americans spend
an average of
17 days fishing
per year.

66

There are only
two occasions when
Americans respect
privacy, especially in
presidents. Those are
prayer and fishing.

99

Oregon-born former US President Herbert Hoover,
who led his country from 1929 to 1933 – and was apt to
remind folk of the need for time alone, whether in
church or by the river.

66

The solution to any problem – work, love, money, whatever – is to go fishing, and the worse the problem, the longer the trip should be.

99

Prolific fishing author and fisherman John Gierach.

"

People often ask why
I fish, and after 70-odd
years, I am beginning
to understand. I fish
because of beauty.

"

The acclaimed angler and angling author
Ernest G. Schwiebert Jr's closing speech at
the American Museum of Fly Fishing
inaugural ceremony (2005).

The oldest known fishing hook dates back 40,000 years, and the practise of eating seafood by humans at least 164,000 years.

"

To go fishing is the chance to wash one's soul with pure air, with the rush of the brook, or with the shimmer of sun on blue water. It brings meekness and inspiration from the decency of nature, charity toward tackle-makers, patience toward fish, a mockery of profits and egos, a quieting of hate, a rejoicing that you do not have to decide a darned thing until next week. And it is discipline in the equality of men – for all men are equal before fish.

"

Herbert Hoover.

66

Whether I caught fish or not,
just the thrill of rolling out that
line and watching my fly turn
over has been good enough for
me. That and the hundreds of
treasured memories I have of
this wonderful sport.

99

Legendary US sportscaster – 'The grandaddy
of them all' – Gowdy (1919-2006) looks back
on many years well spent.

> Fishing gives a man ... some time to collect his thoughts and rearrange them kind of neatly, in an orderly fashion. Once the bait is on the hook and the boat is anchored, there's nothing to interfere with thinking except an occasional bite.

Author and columnist Robert Ruark in his classic novel *The Old Man and the Boy* (1953).

“

I'm a country boy, so
I really appreciate the
country. I love fishing,
so I fish between takes
on set. During lunch,
I go for a fish.

”

Australian actor Travis Fimmel gets his priorities right.

66

And anyone who thinks I brag
in stating that I understand
fish-thought is obviously
ignorant of the way in which
fish think. Believe me, it's
nothing to brag about.

99

Australian TV and radio personality Rex Hunt.

"

For the true angler, fishing
produces a deep,unspoken joy,
born of longing for that which
is quiet and peaceful, and
fostered by an inbred love of
communing with nature.

"

**Thaddeus Norris ("Uncle Thad"), serious fishing fan,
and author of *The American Angler's Book* (1864).**

"

Reading about baseball is a lot more interesting than reading about chess, but you have to wonder: Don't any of these guys ever go fishing?

"

Author unknown.

"

There is only one reason
in the world to go fishing:
to enjoy yourself. Anything
that detracts from enjoying
yourself is to be avoided.

"

The thoughts of Leigh Perkins, the man who turned a
modest tackle shop in Manchester, Vermont into one of
America's most successful lifestyle brands: Orvis.

66

I think it's time for me to get out, because at the moment I'm only thinking about fishing 21 hours a day, and they're the waking moments. And even when I close my eyes I'm thinking about it.

99

**Aussie fishing legend Rex Hunt admits
he's well and truly hooked...**

"

My favourite memories
growing up in North Carolina
were hunting and fishing
with my father and brothers.
There, I developed a deep
appreciation for protecting
land and waterways. There,
I learned outdoorsmanship.

"

Louis Bacon - US billionaire philanthropist,
entrepreneur and founder of Moore Capital Management
- reflects on a treasured childhood.

66

If you like fresh fish, you might like to catch them yourself. That and the fact that fishing has the driving force of a treasure hunt is enough to put you in the stream.

99

Noted author John McPhee in his book
The Founding Fish (2002).

66

Do not tell fish stories where the people know you… but particularly, don't tell them where they know the fish.

99

Mark Twain, the great American humourist, from his collection *More Maxims of Mark* (1927).

66

I think there is a connection
between thinking and fishing,
mostly because you spend a
lot of time up to your waist in
water without a whole lot to
keep your mind busy.

99

US novelist Anthony Doerr reveals the secrets of his
thought process.

Anglers spend
more than
$1 billion a year
on bait alone.

❝

I go fishing not to find myself but to lose myself.

❞

Joseph Monninger, American novelist, shares his
thoughts on his favourite pastime.

66

Give a man a fish and
you feed him for a day.
Teach a man to fish
and you feed him
for a lifetime.

99

Jewish philosopher Moses ben Maimon, more
commonly known as Maimonides (1138-1204), with a
simple observation that is as true now
as it was almost 900 years ago.

"

Give a man a fish and
he will eat for a day.
Teach him how to fish,
and he will sit in a boat
and drink beer all day.

"

Comedian and actor George Carlin has
a more modern take on the classic saying.

"

A trout is a moment of beauty known only to those who seek it.

"

Arnold Gringrich, co-founder and editor of
Esquire **magazine, remarks on his love of fish**
in his book *The Joys of Trout* **(1973).**

66

There is no use in
walking five miles
to fish when you can
depend on being just
as unsuccessful
near home.

99

Mark Twain.

CHAPTER
TWO

Words of Wisdom

Some of the great fishing quotes come from the pens of inspirational writers, theorists and thinkers. Here is a selection of quotes with a literary lean…

"

Somebody behind you
while you are fishing,
is as bad as someone
looking over your
shoulder while you write
a letter to your girl.

"

**One of many great fishing quotes from
Ernest Hemingway that instantly stuck a
chord with millions.**

"

Fishing consists of a series of misadventures interspersed by occasional moments of glory.

"

A line from Howard Marshall's revered classic
Reflections on a River (1967).

66

It's an odd fact of life
that whichever side of
the stream you're on,
two-thirds of the best
water is out of reach
on the other side.

99

John Gierach, author of the cult classic *Trout Bum*
makes this simple observation in his book
No Shortage of Good Days (2011).

"

It is to be observed
that 'angling' is the
name given to fishing
by people who can't fish.

"

Canadian author and humourist Stephen B. Leacock
(1869-1944) succinctly wrote what most fisherman
had been thinking for hundreds of years.

"

The trout do not rise
in the cemetery, so you
better do your fishing
while you are still able.

"

Basically, 'fish while you can', says 'The Dean of
American Fly Fishermen', Sparse Grey Hackle,
also known as Alfred W. Miller.

"

The great charm
of fly fishing is
that we are
always learning.

"

Theodore Gordon.

The five basic methods of angling are bait fishing, fly fishing, bait casting, spinning, and trolling.

> 66

I continually read of men who said they would be just as happy not catching trout as catching them. To me, that even then sounded pious nonsense, and rather more of an excuse than a statement of fact. No, I want to catch them, and every time I slip on my waders and put up a fly, it is with this in mind.

> 99

Brian Clarke, from his bestseller
***The Pursuit of the Stillwater Trout* (1975).**

66

In the mornings, when the grasses were still wet with a bright silver sheen and the antelope fled and the curlew flew ahead of us as we rattled along the rutted and pitted track across the benches down to the river, we always felt the nervous tingling of expectation.

99

Renowned fly fisherman and author Nick Lyons beautifully recalls the anticipation of the day ahead in his book *Spring Creek* (1992).

"

The essentials of a good
fly-hook: The temper of an
angel and penetration of a
prophet; fine enough to be
invisible and strong enough to
kill a bull in a ten-acre field.

"

**Wise words from G.S. Marryat (1840-96)
- better known as 'The Prince of Fly Fishers'.**

"

Time flies so fast after youth is past that we cannot accomplish one half the many things we have in mind. Or indeed one half our duties. The only safe and sensible plan is to make other things give way to the essentials, and the first of these is fly fishing.

"

Theodore Gordon (1854-1915), the 'father of the American school of dry fly fishing' was also a noted writer. This was from one of the many magazine articles he wrote as 'Badger Hackle'.

66

Soon after I embraced the sport of angling I became convinced that I should never be able to enjoy it if I had to rely on the cooperation of the fish.

99

Sparse Grey Hackle,
also known as Alfred W. Miller.

66

Scholars have long known
that fishing eventually turns
men into philosophers.
Unfortunately, it is almost
impossible to buy decent tackle
on a philosopher's salary.

99

Outdoor Life, Field & Stream columnist
Patrick F. McManus (1933-2018)
makes a salient point!

66

We fish for hours
to hold a trout
for seconds.

99

Author unknown.

"

Most fishermen swiftly learn that it's a pretty good rule never to show a favourite spot to any fisherman you wouldn't trust with your wife.

"

Respected lawyer, fly fisherman and author
John D. Voelker (1903-91) clearly kept his favourite
fishing spots to just a few trusted friends.

66

Perhaps I should not
have been a fisherman,
he thought. But that
was the thing that
I was born for.

99

Ernest Hemingway, *The Old Man and the Sea* **(1952).**

"

What a tourist terms a plague of insects, the fly fisher calls a great hatch.

"

Patrick F. McManus.

66

I've gone fishing
thousands of times
in my life, and I have
never once felt unlucky
or poorly paid for those
hours on the water.

99

Bestselling crime writer and fisherman
William Tapply (1940-2009) was also a regular
columnist in *Field and Stream*.

66

Angling is extremely time consuming. That's sort of the whole point.

99

The acclaimed novelist, movie director and outdoor enthusiast Thomas McGuane writes in his epic *The Longest Silence: A Life in Fishing* (2001).

66

Never have I seen
a greater, or more
beautiful, or a calmer
or more noble thing
than you, brother.

99

The character Santiago has more than respect for the
marlin. Ernest Hemingway, from his seminal classic
The Old Man and the Sea (1952).

"

All the romance of trout fishing exists in the mind of the angler and is in no way shared by the fish.

"

Who could argue with Harold F. Blaisdell, the author of so many quality fishing books? This is taken from *The Philosophical Fisherman* (1969).

"

Other fish run
from bigger things.
That's their instinct.
But this fish doesn't
run from anything.
He doesn't fear.

"

Peter Benchley, from his classic 1974 novel *Jaws*.

Five classic fishing books

The Old Man and the Sea
– Ernest Hemingway (1952)

Trout Bum
– John Gierach (1986)

A River Runs Through It
– Norman Maclean (1976)

The River Why
– David James Duncan (1983)

The Longest Silence: A Life in Fishing
– Thomas McGuane (1999)

"

The fish and I were
both stunned and
disbelieving to find
ourselves connected
by a line.

"

William Humphrey, writer, fisherman and author of
My Moby Dick simplifies the moment when an
unforgettable connection is made (1979).

66

In every species of fish I've angled for, it is the ones that have got away that thrill me the most, the ones that keep fresh in my memory. So I say it is good to lose fish. If we didn't, much of the thrill of angling would be gone.

99

Ray Bergman, author of America's bestselling fishing book *Trout* (1938).

"

As no man is born an artist, so no man is born an angler.

"

Izaak Walton, from his classic
The Compleat Angler (1653) -
perhaps the first serious book about fishing.

66

It has always been
my private conviction
that any man who pits
his intelligence against
a fish and loses has
it coming.

99

John Steinbeck, America's most read author, who
enjoyed nothing more than to fish between
creating literary masterpieces.

“

You did not kill the fish only
to keep alive and to sell for
food, he thought. You killed
him for pride and because you
are a fisherman. You loved him
when he was alive and you
loved him after.

”

Ernest Hemingway, *The Old Man and the Sea* (1952).

"

I only hope the fish will take half as much trouble for me as I've taken for them.

"

Poet and novelist Rudyard Kipling (1865-1936) hoped for parity on the riverbank.

"

Fishing books, lit by emotion recollected in tranquillity, are like poetry… We do not think of them as books but as men. They are our companions and not only riverside. Summer and winter they are with us and what a pleasant company they are.

"

Taken from the classic *The Fisherman's Library*, written by *Swallows and Amazons* author Arthur Ransome (1955).

"

There is certainly
something in angling
that tends to produce a
serenity of the mind.

"

Washington Irving (1783-1859), the legendary
American short story writer, historian and biographer,
on his favourite pastime.

66

All Americans believe
that they are born
fishermen. For a man
to admit a distaste for
fishing would be like
denouncing mother-love
or hating moonlight.

99

John Steinbeck.

Practical fishing books

Curtis Creek Manifesto
– Sheridan Anderson (1978)

Field & Stream: The Total Fishing Manual
– Joe Cermele (2013)

Fifty Places to Fly Fish Before you Die
– Chris Santella (2004)

The Bug Book
– Paul Weamer (2016)

How to Think Like a Fish
– Jeremy Wade (2019)

"

Rivers and the inhabitants of the watery element were made for wise men to contemplate and fools to pass without consideration.

"

A gem of an observation from Izaak Walton's
The Compleat Angler (1653).

"

Without sharks, you take away the apex predator of the ocean, and you destroy the entire food chain.

"

Peter Benchley, *Jaws* (1974).

❝

When I told Mary about the project – I mean about researching the possibility of a salmon fishery in the Yemen – something changed.

❞

Paul Torday in *Salmon Fishing in the Yemen*, makes a poignant observation.

CHAPTER
THREE

Man
versus Fish

When it comes down to it,
it is one against the other.
Who is the smarter?
The fish, of course…

" Sharing the fun of fishing turns strangers into friends in a few hours. "

Eugenie Clark.

66

I've never been bitten by a shark, though God knows I had to poke a lot of them in the nose.

99

Scott Glenn, the maverick actor and spear fisherman, reveals his techniques in a *GQ* interview (2016).

Fly fishing is one of the most popular styles of fishing. The Roman Claudius Aelianus wrote of it around 200 CE.

"

If you want to catch more fish, more often, take luck out of your fishing equation and replace it with knowledge of fish, their habitat and behaviour, and you will make your own luck.

"

Sound advice from Tony Bishop, the author of *Fishing Smarter* (1996).

66

It is the curious and inventive angler who, by questioning often long held beliefs, makes us examine our sometimes fixed views.

99

Norman Marsh, the author of *Trout Stream Insects of New Zealand: How to Imitate and Use Them* shares his thoughts on fly fishing (1983).

66

Life is like fishing.
You are rewarded for
your consistency.

99

Author unknown.

66

The chances of that shark attacking you in any way is so remote. The sea should be enjoyed, the animals in it. When you see a shark underwater, you should say, 'How lucky I am to see this beautiful animal in his environment!'

99

Eugenie Clark, 'The Shark Lady' (1922-2015).
Clark was an Ichthyologist and staunch defender
of the most feared fish in the ocean.

66

Interesting fact:
a shark will only
attack you if
you're wet.

99

Just one of the hilarious lines the much-loved UK
comedian Sean Lock (1963–2021) uttered
during his glorious career.

There are
21 million full-
time fishermen
and approximately
200 million people
who depend on
fishing for survival
and livelihood.

66

The issue of imitation has always occupied fly fishers, and part of its endless attraction has been the imponderable uncertainty of how much it matters to the fish in the first place.

99

Paul Schullery, the author of *American Fly Fishing: A History* asks the question most fly fisherman think – but rarely question (1987).

66

You don't have to swim faster than the shark, just faster than the person you're with.

99

Prolific US stand-up and movie actor Kevin Nealon shares some simple advice.

66

Ours is the grandest sport.
It is an intriguing battle of wits
between an angler and a trout;
and in addition to appreciating
the tradition and grace of
the game, we play it in the
magnificent out-of-doors.

99

Expert angler and author Ernest G. Schwiebert, Jr.
(1931-2005) sings the praises of the sport
and the quarry.

"

Wanted: Good woman – Must be able to clean, cook, sew, dig worms and clean fish. Must have boat and motor. Please send picture of boat and motor.

"

**Author unknown
(and probably still in search of a companion).**

"

When I go fishing
I like to know that
there's nobody within
five miles of me.

"

Norman MacCaig (1910-96), the brilliant Scottish poet,
revealed he enjoyed solitude as fisherman.

"

Terry backed up and did a swan dive into the water and was swimming after the fish and the rod. It's the only time I ever saw a fish catch a man.

"

Legendary US sportscaster Curt Gowdy (1919-2006) recalls an unforgettable fishing trip.

"

There are some fish that cannot be caught. It's not that they are faster or stronger than other fish, they're just touched by something extra.

"

Edward Bloom, the fictional character in
Tim Burton's *Big Fish*, says a line that is as true
as the world is round (2003).

Cabo San Lucas, Baja California Sur, Mexico has been nicknamed the "marine capital of the world".

The area has a strict catch-and-release policy, which has helped to boost the population of Marlin. The fishing season goes all year round, but the peak times are between May and December.

"

If you're too successful
to fish whenever you
want, one could argue
that you're not really
a success.

"

Prolific fly fishing author John Gierach's
poignant observation.

66

And finally, I fish not
because I regard fishing as
being terribly important, but
because I suspect that so many
of the other concerns of men
are equally unimportant, and
not nearly so much fun.

99

John D. Voelker.

66

You're gonna need a bigger boat...

99

The immortal line uttered by Amity Island's Chief Brody (Roy Scheider) as he hunts a great white with gnarly sea fishing maverick Quint off the New England coast in the movie *Jaws* (1975).

CHAPTER
FOUR

Hook, Line and Sinker

The act of fishing – on riverbanks, lakesides, streams or the ocean in all weathers has remained popular for hundreds of years. It continues to confound those who haven't (yet) got the bug, but is adored by those who have.

66

The rainbow, the whole
shining body flying up out of
the water, filling me for the first
time, then again and again, with
so much yearning and shock
and recognition and joy that
I can no longer swear I
remained in my body.

99

David James Duncan, the author of *The River Why*,
explains an out-of-body angling experience.

"

Creeps and idiots cannot conceal themselves for long on a fishing trip.

"

Trout Bum author and prolific fly fisherman
John Gierach tells it like it is...

There are more species of fish than mammals, birds, reptiles and amphibians put together, including 70 different species of flying fish alone.

66

Fly tying - The art of attaching
feathers, fur, wool, and silk to
a tiny hook to create artificial
lures that imitate insects, a skill
easily mastered by anyone who
can peel a grape blindfolded
with a pair of tweezers and a
butter knife while wearing
oven mitts.

99

Author unknown.

"

I like night fishing, even
though there is a molecule
of terror in it. Maybe it
is that tiny bit of terror
that I relish, that going
mano a mano with another
predator in the dark.

"

Paul Quinnett, eminent psychologist, author and
veteran fisherman, eloquently describes the thrill
of moonlight angling.

"

To fish well is
to cultivate an
arrangement of
time and place, of
circumstance and
perspective.

"

Prolific fishing author Ted Leeson pretty much nails it
in his excellent *The Habit of Rivers* book (1994).

"

This world needs more tackleboxes and less Xboxes.

"

The country music star Earl Dibbles Jr, real name Granger Smith, makes a poignant observation from his Twitter feed (2013).

"

In the swamp the banks were bare, the big cedars came together overhead, the sun did not come through, except in patches; in the fast deep water, in the half light, the fishing would be tragic.

"

From Ernest Hemingway's 'Big Two-Hearted River' (Parts I and II) featured in his classic *In Our Time* (1925).

"

Many men go fishing all of their lives without knowing that it is not fish they are after.

"

Naturalist and philosopher Henry David Thoreau (1817-62) shares an interesting theory... often interpreted as 'one must live life to its fullest'.

"

In this ever-changing world, there are few things that have remained constant for me. The chance of hooking a nice trout still excites and thrills me to this day... just as it did when I was a kid. I like that!

"

M.A. Bookout, author of *A Glimpse of Freedom*
shares a glimpse of a very happy childhood.

On April 21, 1959, Alfred Dean of Irymple, Victoria caught a 2,664-pound (1,208kg) great white shark off the coast of his native Australia. Amazingly, he subdued this monster – the heaviest record fish ever listed by the International Game Fish Association – in only 50 minutes on 130-pound line.

66

I got 99 problems
and fishin' solves
all of 'em.

99

Earl Dibbles Jr.

"

You've gone out alone before because you were sad or happy, or neither or both – for any reason at all, the way some people drink. The lake is black now, and for a long moment you can't remember why you're here this time.

"

John Gierach tries to explain the automatic pull of fishing in 'Headwaters'. Taken from *Trout Bum* (1986).

❝

Being a dissertation of the symptoms and pathology of this incurable disease by one of its victims.

❞

Robert Traver, the author of *Trout Madness* attempts to describe his own book and fishing addiction (2000).

"

Fishing gives us the opportunity to go to beautiful places and reflect on life.

"

Paul Whitehouse, one half of the hugely successful BBC series *Gone Fishing* sums up his favourite pastime (2021).

66

One thing becomes
clearer as one gets
older and one's fishing
experience increases, and
that is the paramount
importance of one's
fishing companions.

99

Fishing author John Ashley-Cooper's brutally honest
assessment of what is important on the riverbank.

❝

In our family, there was no clear line between religion and fly fishing.

❞

**Norman MacLean's character Norman explains
the blurred line of worship in the semi-autobiographical
book *A River Runs Through It* (1976).**

66

I fake sincerity and pretend to be other people for a living, but with fishing I am me. I feel good about myself and good about the world.

99

Robson Green, British actor and TV presenter of *Extreme Fishing with Robson Green* explains his love of the sport during an interview in *The Daily Mirror* (2018).

66

I love fishing. You put
that line in the water
and you don't know
what's on the other end.
Your imagination is
under there.

99

*M*A*S*H* director and maverick filmmaker
Robert Altman (1925-2006) grasps one of
fishing's great allures – the not knowing!

66

I spent most of my money on fishing. The rest I wasted.

99

Author unknown.

In 1933, Captain Jay Gould of Hollywood, Florida captured a manta ray that measured 19 feet, 9 inches (6 metres) from wing-tip to wing-tip.

The ray was hooked on a large shark hook on 1,200 feet (365 metres) of ½-inch rope. The manta ray's weight was estimated at 5,500 pounds (2,494 kg).

66

I only make
movies to finance
my fishing.

99

Movie star Lee Marvin (1924-87) reveals the real reason
for his prolific Hollywood career...

"

Three-fourths of the Earth's surface is water, and one-fourth is land. It is quite clear that the good Lord intended us to spend triple the amount of time fishing as taking care of the lawn.

"

The legendary US fisherman Chuck Clark has a point!

"

Dear Lord, grant me the
serenity to accept the size of the
fish I catch, the courage not to
lie about it and the wisdom to
know that none of my fishing
buddies would believe me
anyway… Amen.

"

Author unknown.

"

The charm of
fishing is that it is
the pursuit of what is
elusive but attainable,
a perpetual series of
occasions of hope.

"

John Buchan (1875-1940), author of
The Thirty-Nine Steps, explains what angling
meant to him (and most others).

"

An angler is a man
who spends rainy days
sitting around on the
muddy banks of rivers
doing nothing because
his wife won't let him
do it at home.

"

Author unknown.

CHAPTER
FIVE

Deep Waters

The philosophy
of fishing is a subject in itself.
Here are quotes on just that
from the great and the good,
the deep and the not so deep…

66

I don't suppose I ever entirely release a fish. I may not eat it, but that does not mean I take nothing from it before I let it go.

99

Paul Schullery, author of many fine nature and fishing books, lets us in on a secret. Taken from *How Can You Do That?* on flyfisherman.com (2003).

66

Everyone is a genius.
But if you judge a fish
by its ability to climb
a tree, it will live its
whole life believing that
it is stupid.

99

The author of this curious quote is unknown - it is
usually (incorrectly) attributed to Albert Einstein.

"

I thoroughly enjoy getting away from the game and going out fishing because it's so relaxing, so quiet, and peaceful. I mean, there's no noise other than nature… and it's so different from what I do in a tournament situation that it just eases my mind.

"

International golfing champion Tiger Woods.

66

If your concentration is getting bad, take up bass fishing. It will really improve your ability to focus. If you aren't ready when that fish hits, you can't set the hook.

99

Lee Trevino - Veteran US golfer's advice on improving golf - go fishing!

66

There are always new places to go fishing. For any fisherman, there's always a new place, a new horizon.

99

Jack Nicklaus, golfing legend, fisherman extraordinaire.

❝

He finally hooked up, 5 in the afternoon, with this fish. It came out of the water tail-walking, big as a whale. It got dark about 6:30, and he just kept fishing and fishing like in Ernest Hemingway's *The Old Man and the Sea*. He fished forever. Finally, about 11:20, he brought it up. I'm telling you, he fought it for six hours and 20 minutes. One man fought a fish. There was no one other than Jack Nicklaus who could have done it. Or would have.

❞

Golfer Jerry Pate recalls the time he went on an epic sea fishing trip with Jack Nicklaus on the Great Barrier Reef (1978).

66

More than half the intense enjoyment
of fly fishing is derived from
the beautiful surroundings, the
satisfaction felt from being in the
open air, the new lease of life secured
thereby, and the many, many pleasant
recollections of all one has seen,
heard and done.

99

Charles F. Orvis (1831-1915), the founder of
The Orvis Company and a pioneer conservationist.

66

Fishing tournaments seem a little like playing tennis with living balls.

99

Poet and writer James 'Jim' Harrison makes an interesting observation.

"

Fishing is a sport invented by insects and you are the bait.

"

Political satirist and journalist P.J. O'Rourke has an odd take on fishing – not that he's wrong, necessarily.

The act of fishing – for fish, dreams or whatever magic is available – is enough. It transports us to a special world, and a state of mind, where we are free.

Fennel Hudson.

On June 12, 1999, Tiney Mitchell of Port Isabel, Texas, finished constructing the world's largest fly fishing rod and reel.

The rod is a huge 71 feet, 4.5 inches (21.7 metres) long. The reel measures 4 feet (1.2 metres) in diameter and 10 inches (25cm) in width.

"

If I fished only to capture
fish, my fishing trips
would have ended long ago.

"

Bestselling author and frequent fisherman Zane Grey,
from his book *Tales of Southern Rivers* (1924).

"

Having a fishing rod in your hand is merely an excuse to explore out-of-sight depths and reveal mysteries that previously only existed in dreams.

"

Author Nigel 'Fennel' Hudson, angling, countryside author, and broadcaster. He's best known for the *Fennel's Journal* series of books and as host of 'The Contented Countryman' podcast.

66

A fish only begins to realize its potential the moment you throw it in deep waters.

99

Canadian philosopher Matshona Dhliwayo's interesting theory...

"

When you fish
for love, bait with
your heart, not
your brain.

"

Mark Twain.

66

Sell a man a fish, he eats for a day, teach a man how to fish, you ruin a wonderful business opportunity.

99

Karl Marx (1818-83) the great philosopher with a line Groucho Marx would have been proud of!

"

Having a fishing rod
in your hand is merely
an excuse to explore
out-of-sight depths and
reveal mysteries that
previously only existed
in dreams.

"

Fennel Hudson.

66

The two biggest things that translate
from a pitching mound to hunting
and fishing are patience and
perseverance. When you're on the
mound, you have to take the game one
pitch at a time, regardless of the score,
and that approach helps when I'm in
the woods or out on the water as well.

99

Jon Lester, veteran baseball pitcher for the
St. Louis Cardinals and keen fisherman,
taking it one fish at a time.

66

Fishing is a condition of the mind wherein one cannot have a bad time.

99

Bestselling author and frequent fisherman Zane Grey.

“

Fishing provides that connection
with the whole living world. It gives
you the opportunity of being totally
immersed, turning back into yourself
in a good way. A form of meditation,
some form of communion with levels
of yourself that are deeper than the
ordinary self.

”

**Poet Laureate Ted Hughes (1930-88) with a
typically profound observation.**

Best estimates by scientists
place the number of fish
in the ocean at
3,500,000,000,000,
a number is constantly
changing due to factors
such as predation,
fishing, reproduction, and
environmental state.

World Atlas (2021).

66

The true angler can welcome even a low river and a dry year, and learn of it, and be the better for it, in mind and in spirit.

99

Historian, poet and novelist G.M.W. Wemyss on how fishing can cleanse one's soul.

66

I object to fishing
tournaments less for
what they do to fish
than what they do
to fishermen.

99

**Former Boston Red Sox left fielder and renowned fly
fisherman Ted Williams (1918-2002) on the unpleasantly
competitive nature of angling competitions.**

"

We ask a simple
question and that is
all we wish: Are all
fishermen liars or do
only liars fish?

"

Canadian academic William Sherwood Fox (1878-1967)
tries to solve an age-old perception...

CHAPTER
SIX

The Ones That Got Away

Tall tales, simple one-liners and
so-fish-ticated sentence…

66

Everyone should believe in something. I believe I'll go fishing.

99

Naturalist and philosopher Henry David Thoreau
(1817-62) shares his beliefs.

66

Fly fishing is like sex, everyone thinks there is more than there is, and that everyone is getting more than their share.

99

Henry Kanemoto, Wisconsin doctor and fly fishing enthusiast, keeps things real (1996).

An old man on his deathbed
calls in his family and says,
"I must apologize to you all.
I suppose I haven't been the
perfect father and husband.
I shamefully admit that I spent
as much of my life as I could on
the water. I was rarely at home
during the fishing seasons and
I'll admit that I spent too much
time at the tackle shop, and too
much money on rods

and lines and reels." He pauses
there to rest for a minute, then
continues, "I've been a terrible
father and I hope you all forgive
me." Then he pauses again and
looks around. He closes his
eyes, smiles and says in a half-
whisper to himself, "But on the
other hand… I have caught a
helluva lot of fish."

Author unknown.

66

The two best times to fish is when it's rainin' and when it ain't.

99

Outdoor Life, Field & Stream columnist
Patrick F. McManus (1933-2018) was clearly
an 'any weather' sort of guy.

66

Fishing is a quest for
knowledge and wonder as much
as a pursuit of fish.

99

Author Paul Schullery.

"

Fly fishermen are born honest, but they get over it.

"

Ed Zern (1920-94), a conservationist, writer, humourist and fisherman.

66

I fish better with
a lit cigar; some
people fish better
with talent.

99

**Nick Lyons, author of *Bright Rivers* on the secret
of his success (2014).**

"

Game fish are too valuable to be caught only once.

"

Artist, pilot, fly fisherman, author, filmmaker, outfitter and conservationist Lee Wulff made significant contributions to recreational fishing, especially fly fishing and the conservation of Atlantic Salmon.

66

The finest gift you can
give to any fisherman
is to put a good fish
back, and who knows if
the fish that you caught
isn't someone else's
gift to you?

99

Lee Wulff.

"

For the fish, the lake in which
he lives is the universe. What
does the fish think when he is
jerked up by the mouth through
the silver limits of existence
and into a new universe where
the air drowns him and the
light is blue madness?

"

Stephen King, the master of horror, writing in
The Dark Tower: The Gunslinger (1982).

66

Early to bed
Early to rise
Fish all day
Make up lies.

99

Author unknown.

"

Last year I went
fishing with Salvador
Dali. He was using a
dotted line. He caught
every other fish.

"

Legendary US stand-up comic Steven Wright with his own unique take on fishing.

66

There is a fine
line between
fishing and just
standing on the
shore like an idiot.

99

Steven Wright.

"

I fished upstream coming ever closer and closer to the narrow staircase of the canyon. Then I went up into it as if I were entering a department store. I caught three trout in the lost and found department.

"

Richard Brautigan, from his book
Trout Fishing in America (1988).

66

Bragging may not
bring happiness, but
no man having caught
a large fish goes home
through an alley.

99

Ann Landers, the powerful *Chicago Sun-Times*
columnist, makes a salient point!

66

A worm is a small, reluctant animal used to capture a larger reluctant animal.

99

Author unknown.

66

I don't want to sit at the head table anymore. I want to go fishing.

99

George H W Bush (1924-2018) the 41st President of the
US looks forward to a life less taxing (1993).

66

Many of the most highly
publicized events of
my presidency are not
nearly as memorable or
significant in my life as
fishing with my daddy.

99

**A poignant admission from Jimmy Carter,
the 39th President of the US.**

"

So Long, and Thanks for All the Fish.

"

Douglas Adams' memorable title for the fourth book of the *Hitchhikers' Guide to the Galaxy series* (1984).

"

Calling fishing a hobby is like calling brain surgery a job.

"

Renowned fly fishing author Paul Schullery (correctly) suggests there is more to fishing than meets the eye...

66

Of all the liars
among mankind,
the fisherman
is the most
trustworthy.

99

William Sherwood Fox.

"

I didn't think I had time for fishing before I fished.

"

**Comedian and *Gone Fishing* co-star
Bob Mortimer, taking a gentler approach to life
after his open-heart surgery (2019).**

"

Nothing makes
a fish bigger
than almost
being caught.

"

Author unknown.

"

The fly angler who says they have never, ever fallen while wading is either a pathogenic liar, or has never been fly fishing.

"

Acclaimed fishing author Jimmy Moore casts aspersions!

66

My biggest worry is that my wife (when I'm dead) will sell my fishing gear for what I said I paid for it.

99

Koos Brandt, the US multi-millionaire, expecting to have some explaining to do in the afterlife.

66

Fishing is such great fun, I have often felt, that it really ought to be done in bed.

99

John D. Voelker.

66

You know the thing I liked
about fishing when I was
14 was being out with your
mates mucking about, throwing
bread around, getting a bit
wet, maybe. I wondered if that
could be the same when you
were 60. And it didn't feel
that different…

99

Bob Mortimer (2018).

❝

Men and fish are alike. They both get into trouble when they open their mouths.

❞

Author unknown.

66

If people concentrated
on the really important
things in life, there'd
be a shortage of
fishing poles.

99

Doug Larson (1926-2017) with a typically
astute observation.

"

Most of the world
is covered by water.
A fisherman's job is
simple: Pick out the
best parts.

"

**Charles F. Waterman, prolific fishing author,
offers simple, effective advice!**

66

I know I fish too
much; so from now on
I will only fish on days
ending with Y.

99

Author unknown.

"

Fishing, with me, has always been an excuse to drink in the daytime.

"

Legendary sports journalist Jimmy Cannon (1900-73) raises a glass to fishing.

66

Brown trout, speckled cunning, a fox with fins.

99

Talented New Zealand-based artist and trout fisherman Martin Simpson captures the spirit of the brown trout perfectly.

"

I love fishing. It's transcendental meditation with a punchline.

"

Scottish comedian Billy Connolly has obviously spent many moments alone on the banks of a river (or loch).

Always think like a fish, no matter how weird it gets.

Author unknown.

"

Fish come in three sizes: small, medium and the one that got away.

"

Author unknown.

"

Fishing adds years to your life, and life to your years.

"

Poignant comment from revered author and *Bassmaster Magazine* columnist Homer Circle (1915-2012).

"

Gone fishin', be back at dark-thirty!

"

Author unknown.

"

Fishing is not
an escape from life,
but often a deeper
immersion into it.

"

Outstanding fishing writer Harry Middleton (1949-93),
discovered by many long after his untimely passing.

66

Fishing, by its very nature, nourishes the imagination, feeding it with a potent fuel of hope and desire.

99

Tony Bishop.